Called to Pastor
Now What?
Be the Pastor Your Church Needs

Roy W. Harris

RHM

Contents

Introduction

Pastoring in today's world is complicated and challenging.

I well remember answering God's call to pastor my first church in Ahoskie, North Carolina. I was excited and also a little nervous. I was called to be a pastor, but I wondered, "Now how do I do the job?"

Those early days were filled with excitement, anticipation, and the desire to be a good pastor to my people. I learned lessons each day about my people and what I needed to do that day.

This book is a collection of key lessons I learned that helped me become successful in pastoring five churches over the past 40 years. The book is filled with practical, organized and systematic ways of fulfilling pastoral responsibilities. I truly believe it can be a tremendous asset to rookie and veteran pastors alike.

Love Your Congregation

1 Corinthians 13:1-8 - *If I speak in the tongues of men and of angels, but have not love, I am a noisy gong or a clanging cymbal. And if I have prophetic powers, and understand all mysteries and all knowledge, and if I have all faith, so as to remove mountains, but have not love, I am nothing. If I give away all I have, and if I deliver up my body to be burned, but have not love, I gain nothing. Love is patient and kind; love does not envy or boast; it is not arrogant or rude. It does not insist on its own way; it is not irritable or resentful; it does not rejoice at wrongdoing, but rejoices with the truth. Love bears all things, believes all things, hopes all things, and endures all things. Love never ends.*

A family was in a serious traffic accident. The youngest son, Mike, was seriously injured and needed blood. His big brother, Danny, was only 8 years old, but had the same blood type. Danny's dad carefully explained how important it was for Mike to receive blood, and how great it would be if Danny could help Mike by giving him some of his blood.

There was silence, and then Danny said, *Yes, Daddy, I'll give my blood so Mike can get better.* They put the needle in his vein and drew the blood they needed. Once the needle was removed, Danny looked up at his Dad, and with tears running down his cheeks said...

I will finish the story at the end of the chapter.

Congregations want their pastors to love them. They want to be loved individually and collectively, and they know if their pastors love them. They will remember more about how their pastors loved them than the great things the pastors accomplished.

How can pastors love their congregations?

1.　*Serve with joy.* It has been said that *if you enjoy your job, you will never work a day in your life.* There is much truth in that statement. Churches want pastors who enjoy pastoring and, in particular, enjoy being their pastor. Pastors who have lost their joy in serving will eventually lose the churches they serve.

2.   *Listen carefully when they speak.*
Individuals should feel that their pastor is giving them undivided attention and that they are important and valuable in his eyes. Let them tell you their stories.

3.   *Listen for what they may not be telling you.* People sometimes talk with pastors about one thing when there is actually something else going on with them. Pastors should be sensitive when individuals are concerned, upset or distressed. They should carefully attempt to explore a little deeper. Many times people will eventually share what is really on their hearts.

4. *Laugh with them.* Congregations love pastors with a sense of humor. Laughing and times of lightheartedness communicate a side of pastors that congregations need to see. It helps people feel that the pastor is one of them.

5. *Cry with them.* Pastors who show their tender compassionate side connect with their people in a special way. Congregations tend to be more open and transparent with their pastors if they feel their pastors are hurting with and for them. Many times they only

need the pastor to listen and empathize with them. One important way congregations know their pastors love them is when they are there for them and with them during the hard, tragic, sorrowful and difficult times in their lives.

6. *Forgive them when they hurt one another.* Pastors must remember that there are always two sides to every story and situation. Pastors should be short on placing blame and long on reconciliation in trying to help their people get along with each other. Taking sides will make the pastor a hero to one member, but could create bad feelings from another. Pastors should attempt to mediate and bring people together. That is not always possible, but the pastor must remember that he is the pastor of all concerned. He must also remember that his people are imperfect creatures who make mistakes, and he must forgive them for their shortcomings and love them despite their faults.

7. *Do not take it personally when they hurt you.* I remember a two-year-old, cute little blond-haired girl from our church who passed away in her sleep one night. I received a call at 3:00 a.m. that no

pastor wants to receive. I hurried to our nearby hospital, and her grandfather met me at the emergency room entrance. *She's dead! What kind of God would kill my granddaughter?* he screamed at me.

I remained silent and spent the next hour or so with the family in a private conference room. The grandfather was angry with everyone and everything at that moment. His hurt and grief came out in words for which he later apologized to me.

People are sometimes immature and hurtful, and they will say things that hurt pastors. Pastors must rise above the hurt and not hold grudges or harbor hurt feelings towards their congregations. They should do their best not to take it personally. They cannot be effective pastors if they cannot learn to forgive and forget the mistakes of the people to whom they minister.

8.   *Privately and publicly commend your people.* People want and need to know they are appreciated. Pastors would do well to be generous with credit in recognizing the hard work of their people. A *thank you* or *well done* expressed privately with individuals makes them feel special and

important to the pastor. Publicly thanking people by name shows recognition and appreciation, and it engenders a desire in others to stay involved and do even more.

9.   *Pray for your people.* Most pastors recognize the value and importance of prayer. Praying for each member demonstrates a keen interest in what is happening in each member's life.

I began a practice that helped me greatly in praying for my people. I prayed for them in the church sanctuary. I knew where each member sat during our services. I would begin with the front rows and pray for each member who sat on those rows. I would then move down the aisle from front to back and from row to row praying for each individual on each row. I would continue this until I reached the final row, having prayed for every person who attended our services. In addition, I kept a list of our shut-ins, and those in hospitals and nursing homes, and I prayed for them as well.

10.   *Pray with your people.* People turn to pastors for comfort, encouragement and help. A good policy is to let parishioners share their feelings and

stories while listening carefully with compassionate ears. Pastors will not always have the answer, but they do always have something to offer. You have the love of Christ and the power of prayer to share. I have often asked individuals, *Would you mind if I pray for you about this situation right now?*

Praying with your people is one of the greatest things you can do for them. Beseeching the God of the universe on their behalf for His intervention, help and power tremendously encourages them. They are reminded that God loves them, is keenly aware of what is going on in their lives, has the power to do something about it and wants to be involved in their lives and situations.

11.   *Preach the truth to your people.* The pastor's primary responsibility is to preach the Word of God. He must be true to that Word and preach it without reservation or apology. Your people deserve and want you to preach to them. They want you to be faithful in studying the Word and faithful in delivering the Word to them. They want to know what the Word says, how it affects them, how they should respond and how they should live. Loving your people requires *not shrinking back from preaching the whole counsel*

of God, as mentioned in Acts 20:27.

12. *Call your people by their names.* Pastors should be diligent in learning each person's name in their congregations. Parishioners feel much closer to their pastors when their pastors call them by name. They feel their pastor knows who they are and that they are valuable in his eyes.

13. *Love everyone.* This seems like a given, but I think it needs mentioning. Pastors should attempt to love every person in every age group. Some people are easier to love than others, but pastors must do their best to love even those who are less lovable.

Infants, toddlers, preschoolers, elementary school children, middle schoolers, teenagers, college-age individuals, young adults, middle-aged adults, and older people all need to be loved by their pastor. I enjoy holding infants and toddlers and making them smile. I love to engage elementary children by finding out who their teachers are and if they are enjoying school. With middle school children, I often ask if they are playing sports or what their favorite subject is. I developed a special handshake that I use with middle and high school children. I tell each child that I only share that handshake with special people and that they are one of those special people.

I talk with young adults about college, jobs, and dating. I engage middle age adults about their careers, family, etc. I discuss with my older people about their retirement, children, health, etc. Young and old alike should feel the pastor knows their names, who they are, and that he is interested in and loves them.

14.   *Be there for your people when they are ill, serving as caregivers, and grieving.* Those are some of the most traumatic times in people's lives. They look to their pastor for encouragement, a shoulder to cry on and someone to lean on. They may feel freer to share their hearts and feelings with their pastors than with family members and friends. They must believe, even before they need him, that their pastor will be there.

15.   *Apologize when you make mistakes.* Pastors are human and make mistakes. Do not let your pride keep you from saying *I'm sorry*. A simple

apology may defuse a situation that might catch fire and get out of hand. You may misread a situation or a person's action. When you blow it, admit it! The sooner you face it, the better for everyone involved.

Apologize, even when it is not your fault. I have apologized for things I did not do. You might wonder, why? If it appeared to me that an individual believed I had said or done something that hurt their feelings or offended them, then I apologized. Perception is reality to most people.

There are exceptions when it comes to your character being challenged or being accused of immoral conduct or outright sin. We should always stand for that which is right based on the truth of the Word of God.

16. *Maintain proper boundaries.*
Congregations have a tendency to put pastors on pedestals and view them as almost perfect, never making mistakes. Pastors must be careful not to become too close to parishioners.

Spending too much time with an individual or family may give the appearance that you favor them above other members of the congregation. There is also a danger that the individual or family might misunderstand the extra attention. Love everyone equally.

17. *Tell your people that you love them.* You know it. They may know it. But it is important that you tell them often. Just as husbands and wives should often reaffirm their love for each other, congregations and pastors should reassure each other that their relationship is solid. The pastor is the key. He must remind members over and over again of his love and loyalty. Statements like: *I'm so thankful for you, I appreciate you, thank you for loving me and my family, I want you to know how much my wife and I love you,* and *this church means the world to me* will bring smiles to your people's faces and warmth to their hearts.

18. *Know when it is time to leave.* Just as the Holy Spirit gave you the green light to accept the church and become its pastor, He will also give you a flashing light in your soul indicating your time as their pastor is coming to an end.

Leave when it is time to leave. Loving your people demands it. Staying too long will probably cause the relationship to decline.

19.   Your people may not remember much about how you arrived, but they will remember how you leave. Leave on a positive note, even if you have been hurt or wronged. If you exhibit anger or become the victim, then that will be the memory that will stay with your people.

Leave with your head held high, thanking God for the wonderful things He has done with and through your ministry while their pastor. If you leave on a positive note, your people will remember you in a positive way and will reflect on the good things that were accomplished through your ministry while you were their pastor.

Back to our story….

A family was in a terrible traffic accident. The youngest son, Mike, was seriously injured and had lost a lot of blood. His big brother Danny was only 8 years old but had the same blood type.

Danny's dad explained carefully to Danny how important it was for Mike to receive blood, and how great it would be if Danny could help Mike by giving him some of his blood. Danny was very quiet and then he said, *Yes, Daddy, I'll give my blood so Mike can get better*.

18

They placed the needle in Danny's vein and the blood began to flow down the long tube into the sterile plastic container. Danny looked up at his Dad as the needle was being removed, with tears running down his cheeks said, *Daddy, when do I die?*

It was only then that his dad realized that Danny did not know he was just giving some blood. He thought he was giving his life for his brother. Jesus said in John 15:13 *Greater love has no one than this; that someone lay down his life for his friends.* Danny did not understand the full ramifications of his commitment to give his blood, but he assumed it required giving all he had, his life.

Pastors may not understand all the ramifications of the commitment to love their people, but they must understand that commitment requires them to give the best they have. Becoming the pastor every church wants requires truly loving people, and especially their congregations.

Do you want to become the pastor your church wants and needs? Love your people!

Exhibit Good Character

1 Timothy 3:2 - *An overseer must be above reproach, the husband of one wife, sober-minded, self-controlled, respectable, hospitable and able to teach.*

Churches understand that no pastor is perfect, but they want a pastor whose character is above reproach on personal, moral, family and financial levels.

One dark night after 11 p.m., an older African American woman was standing on the side of a highway in the middle of a terrible rainstorm. Her car had broken down and she desperately needed help. She was soaking wet and decided to flag down the next car that came along.

A young white man stopped to help her. This was almost unheard of in those conflict-filled days of the 1960s. The man gave her a ride, took her to safety and helped her get the assistance she needed. She thanked him but seemed preoccupied and in a hurry. She asked him for his address and scribbled it down on a scrap piece of paper.

You will never guess what happened seven days later. It truly is almost unbelievable, and I will tell you the rest of the story at the end of the chapter.

Good character attracts the trust and respect of others; it allows one to influence people in positive ways. Good character changes one's perspective on success and failure, and it sustains through times of opposition. Good character improves self-esteem, self-respect, and self-confidence and is the foundation for happy and healthy relationships. Finally, good character helps one stay committed to his or her core values and goals and improves the chances for success in life.

I am not sure when or where I first heard this, but I believe it is true: *Character is who you are when no one is watching.* Below are some good character traits that churches want pastors to possess.

1. Integrity

What is integrity? Integrity is the possession of strong moral principles, based on deep core values and reliance on those principles to guide us in the way we live our lives. When we have integrity, we remain

---

true to our principles, regardless of whether others are watching.

2. Honesty

Honesty is more than just telling the truth; it is living the truth. Honesty means being transparent and trustworthy in all our relationships, actions and thoughts. We must remember, telling a *half-truth* is tantamount to telling a *whole lie*.

3. Loyalty

Loyalty means being faithful and devoted to family and friends. It also involves being faithful to employers, organizations and communities.

4. Respect

Respect includes treating yourself and others with kindness, courtesy and dignity. Respect is a sign of valuing the worth of others by accepting who they are, including their flaws and imperfections.

5. Responsibility

Responsibility entails the acceptance of personal, relationship, career, community, and society obligations, even when they are difficult, inconvenient or uncomfortable. Responsibility requires following through on commitments. It demands accountability for personal behavior, organizational choices and completetion of tasks. Wise pastors learn early to accept responsibility rather than shift blame for mistakes to others.

6. Humility

What is humility? One person said, *When people believe they have achieved humility, they just lost it*.

Humility means having a confident, yet modest opinion of one's own self-importance. One does not see himself or herself as better than other people or too important to become involved in unpleasant situations. Humility is a heart-felt attitude of gratitude for who one is and how one has been blessed rather than a feeling of entitlement and dissatisfaction.

7. Compassion

Compassion is a feeling of deep sympathy and pity for the suffering and misfortune of others and a desire to help ease their suffering.

8. Fairness

Fairness involves using integrity, compassion,

and discernment in making decisions. It involves taking the best course of action based on the best outcome for everyone involved.

9. Forgiveness

Forgiveness comprises making a conscious and intentional decision to let go of resentment and anger toward someone for an offense, even if the offender does not seek forgiveness. Forgiveness may include pardon, reconciliation and restoration. It extends to others and to one's self.

10. Authenticity

Churches want pastors to be real. They want pastors who are sincere and true to who they are, without pretending to be something they are not. They want pastors who are able to show that they are vulnerable at times and are also aware of their strengths and weaknesses.

11. Courage

Courage involves moving forward with mental stamina to carry out a decision, commitment, plan or decision regardless of fear, danger, discomfort or pain, because it is the right and best course of action.

12. Generosity

Generosity is the willingness to offer freely and often of one's time, energy, effort, emotions, words, and assets without expecting something in return.

13. Perseverance

Perseverance is the steadfast determination to continue with a course of action, belief, or purpose, even if it is difficult or uncomfortable in order to reach a higher goal or outcome. It means seeing it through and refusing to quit.

14. Politeness

Politeness is the use of basic good manners, extending common courtesies and showing proper etiquette to all people. Learning to be polite warms relationships and enhances self-esteem.

15. Kindness

Kindness involves showing an attitude of consideration, helpfulness, and benevolence to others. It comes from a positive disposition with a desire for pleasant interaction with others.

16. Love

Love for others is the ability to express that feeling through words and actions. It requires the willingness to be open and vulnerable.

17. Optimism

Optimism is a sense of hopefulness and confidence about the future. It involves a positive mental attitude in which life events, people, and situations are viewed in a promising light.

18. Reliability

Reliability is the characteristic of being consistent and dependable to follow through on commitments, actions, and decisions. A reliable person will do what was promised.

19. Conscientious

Conscientiousness is the desire to do things well and to the best of one's ability. The conscientious person is thorough, organized, efficient, and vigilant, guided by principle and a sense of what is right.

20. Self-discipline

Self-discipline is the ability to overcome

personal desires and feelings through well-established good habits and willpower. This results in staying true to one's principles, rising to fulfill commitments, and opting to follow the apparent best course of action. A strong sense of self-control produced by self-discipline is necessary in order to reach important and desired goals.

Back to our story...

One dark night after 11 p.m., an older African American woman was standing on the side of a highway in the middle of a terrible rainstorm. Her car had broken down, and she desperately needed help. She was soaking wet and decided to flag down the next car that came along.

A young white man stopped to help her. This was almost unheard of in those conflict-filled days of the 1960s. The man gave her a ride, took her to safety and helped get the assistance she needed.

She thanked him but seemed preoccupied and in a hurry. She asked him for his address and scribbled it down on a scrap piece of paper.

Seven days went by, and then came a knock on the man's door. To his surprise, a giant flat screen television was delivered to his home. A special note was attached. The note read: *Thank you so much for assisting me on the highway the other night. The rain drenched not only my clothes, but also my spirits. Then you came along. Because of you, I was able to make it to my dying husband's bedside just before he passed away. God bless you for helping me and unselfishly serving others.* Sincerely, Mrs. Nat King Cole.

The man who stopped that night to help Mrs. Cole was truly a man of good character. He demonstrated several of the good character traits mentioned above.

What kind of pastors do churches want? They want pastors with good character. Churches want pastors who possess and demonstrate good character every day, in every situation. Not only do churches want this, but God also expects it from those who would shepherd His sheep.

Let us return to where we began in this chapter with Paul instructing young Timothy in 1 Timothy 3:2, *An overseer must be above reproach, the husband of one wife, sober-minded, self-controlled, respectable, hospitable and able to teach.*

What kind of pastor do churches want? They want pastors with good character!

Model Good Leadership

Mark 10:42-45 *And Jesus called them to him and said to them, you know that those who are considered rulers of the Gentiles lord it over them, and their great ones exercise authority over them. But it shall not be so among you. But whoever would be great among you must be your servant, and whoever would be first among you must be slave of all. Even the Son of Man came not to be served but to serve, and to give his life as a ransom for many.* (ESV)

Here is one deacon's observation about his church's pastors: *Most of the pastors in my church have demonstrated a good balance; they have been strong leaders but not dictators.*

I am sure you have heard the expression, *He or she is a born leader,* or possibly *Leaders are made, not born.* Well, which is it?

Some people seem to be born with a God-given ability to lead others, while sometimes it seems the most unlikely people develop into exceptional leaders. The truth may be somewhere in between. Good leadership probably requires some of both.

The morning had been a successful one, with several men and women arriving early for a spruce-up day around the church. The 75-year-old prize dogwood tree stood tall in all its glory in front of the church. Our congregation considered the tree almost a monument, especially when its broad canopy presented a beautiful backdrop when in full bloom.

We had developed plans to build a new sanctuary, and it would sit on the exact spot where the dogwood was growing. I was working in the yard with the others when a matter came to my attention, so I stepped into my office. The office window was open, and I heard a voice calling me from the other side of the window screen. It was Bill (not his real name.) *Pastor,* he said, *that dogwood tree is hard to mow under. One day I'm going to come by and cut it back so it won't keep hitting me in the face every time I try to mow under it.*

The tree needed trimming and I was glad to hear that Bill was willing to tackle it. I told Bill that would be great and to let me know when he wanted to do it and I would help him.

I remained in my office, and about thirty minutes later Bill stepped through the door. You will never guess what told me. I will finish this true story at the end of this chapter.

Good leadership requires knowledge, experience, and wisdom. There are certain important qualities that seem to be present in successful leaders. Below is a list of some of those qualities.

Important Qualities That Make A Great Leader

1. *Honesty* – I mentioned this in the last chapter but I wanted to emphasize and expand on it here. When you are responsible for people, it is important to raise the bar for your own behavior even higher. Your people are a reflection of you, and if you make honest and ethical behavior a key value, your people will follow suit.

Preach and teach your core values and beliefs and post them in your office. Encourage your people to live up to these standards. By emphasizing these standards and displaying them yourself, you will hopefully create an environment that is a friendly, happy, and helpful place to worship and serve for your people.

2. Ability to Delegate - If you do not learn to trust your people with your vision, you may never progress to the next stage in implementing the vision. It is important to remember that trusting your congregation with your idea is a sign of strength, not weakness. Delegating tasks to capable people is one of the most important skills you can develop as your church grows.

Ministerial tasks will begin to pile up, and the more you stretch yourself thin, the lower your quality of work will become, and the less you will produce. The key to delegation is identifying the strengths of your people and capitalizing on them. Find out what each of your people enjoys doing. If they find a task enjoyable, they will likely put more thought and effort into it. This will not only prove that you trust and believe in them, but it will also free up your time to focus on higher level responsibilities that should not be delegated. It is a delicate balance, but one that will have a huge impact on your productivity as pastor.

3. Ability to Communicate - Knowing what you want accomplished may seem clear in your head, but if you try to explain it to someone else and are met with a blank expression, you know there is a problem. If this has been your experience, then you may want to focus on honing your communication skills. Being able to clearly and succinctly describe what you want done is extremely important. If you cannot relate your vision to your people, you will not be working towards the same goals.

Good morale is important, and it is your job as the leader to project a positive atmosphere and not be a point of negativity with your people. A great sense of humor will pay off in huge dividends with your people. Encourage your congregation to laugh. If you are constantly learning to find humor in the struggles of ministry, your work environment will become a happy and healthy space where your people look forward to coming to church and serving in ministry, rather than dreading it.

4.   *Confidence* – There may be days that things do not seem to be going exactly the way you had hoped. This is true with any church. The most important thing is not to panic. Part of your job as a leader is to put out fires and maintain good morale. Keep up your confidence level. Reassure everyone that setbacks are normal and that the important thing is to focus on the larger goal. Staying calm and

confident will keep your people feeling calm and confident. Remember, your congregation will take cues from you. If you exhibit a level of calm damage control, your people will pick up on that feeling. The key objective is to keep everyone engaged and moving forward.

5.   *Commitment* – You must lead by example if you expect your team to work hard and produce quality content. There is no greater motivation than seeing the pastor down in the trenches working alongside everyone else, showing that hard work is being done on every level.

By proving your commitment to your people and your role as their pastor, you will not only earn the respect of your team but will also instill that same hardworking energy among your church leadership team. It is important to show your commitment to the work at hand and to keep promises. If you pledge to do something, then do it. Keep your word!

You want to be known as a fair leader. Once you have gained the respect of your people, they are more likely to follow you wherever you want to take them.

6.   *Creativity* – Some decisions will not always be clear-cut. You may be forced to deviate from your set course and make an immediate decision. This is where your creativity will prove to be vital. Your people will look to you during these critical situations for guidance, and you may be forced to make that quick decision.

It is important to learn to think outside the box and to choose which of two difficult choices seems to be the best option. Do not immediately choose the first or easiest possibility. It is best to take time to think about the situation and consult your leadership team for input and guidance. You can typically reach the good conclusion you were aiming for by looking at all the possible options before deciding too quickly.

7.   *Intuition* - When leading through uncharted waters, there is no roadmap on what to do. Everything is uncertain and the higher the risk, the higher the pressure. That is when you will have to depend on your natural intuition. Guiding through the process of day-to-day routine can be almost turned into a science. However, when something unexpected occurs or you are thrown into a new scenario, people will look to you for guidance. Drawing on past

experience is a good reflex. So is reaching out to your leadership team for support. Eventually, the tough decisions will be up to you to make and you will need to depend on your gut instinct and the Lord for answers. Learning to trust in yourself is as important as your people learning to trust you.

8.   *Inspiration* - Inspiring your congregation to see your vision of what is to come and making them feel invested in the success of the ministry is vital. Generating enthusiasm for hard work is important. Being able to inspire your people will help them focus on the future goals. It is your job to keep spirits up, and that begins with an appreciation for hard work.

9.   *Approach* - Something that is often overlooked is that all human beings are not the same. People come pre-conditioned with various cultural perspectives, language barriers, educational backgrounds, personality traits, and value systems. All of these factors greatly affect how individuals process and interpret information. Some people work well under pressure and others do not. You must adapt your approach on a person-by-person basis, keeping

in mind the situation at hand in order to maximize your effectiveness as a leader.

Back to our story...

The morning had been a successful one with several men and women arriving early for a spruce up day around the church.

The 75-year-old prize dogwood tree stood tall in all its glory in front of the church. Our congregation considered the tree almost a monument, especially when its broad canopy presented a beautiful backdrop when in full bloom.

We had developed plans to build a new sanctuary and it would sit on the exact spot where the dogwood was growing. I was working in the yard with the others when a matter came to my attention, so I stepped into my office. The office window was open, and I heard a voice calling me from the other side of the window screen. It was Bill (not his real name). *Pastor,* he said, *that dogwood tree is hard to mow under. One day I'm going to come by and cut it back so it won't keep hitting me in the face every time I try to mow under it.*

The tree needed trimming, and I was glad to hear that Bill was willing to tackle it. I told Bill that would be great and to let me know when he wanted to trim it and I would help him.

I remained in my office, and about thirty minutes later Bill walked in. *Pastor,* he said, *I took care of that tree. It won't be hitting anyone in the face again*! I felt a sick feeling sweep over me as I turned around in my chair and looked out the window. The feeling was justified! I felt the blood drain from my face all the way down to my feet.

Bill had butchered the tree. The beautiful age-old monument looked like a pitiful abused bush. I knew both Bill and I were in big trouble. Tomorrow was Sunday, and I could almost hear the voices of an irate congregation bemoaning the terrible act that had just occurred.

Sunday arrived and my worst fears were realized. One after another, the complaints came. *Pastor, what it in the world did you do to our tree?* was pretty much the gist of them. Some said it calmly, while others said it with angry faces and raised voices. Needless to say, worship that day was cold and there was terrible dissention in the camp. I went home from church about as discouraged as I had ever been. I was not sure I could survive this situation and remain as pastor.

Our monthly deacons' meeting was already scheduled for that afternoon. We met in my office. Soon after the meeting began, one of my deacons asked, *Pastor, have you had any comments about the dogwood tree?* They knew basically what had happened and that it was not my fault. I sought their counsel on what we should do. My youngest deacon said, *Pastor, we voted to cut the tree down to build our new sanctuary. I would suggest it be gone before Wednesday evening Bible study. If it remains, it will a constant reminder, and folks will be slow to get past it.*

They agreed to support me, and I made sure the tree was down by Wednesday. I talked to Bill that evening after our service and we agreed to meet the next day to take the tree down and remove it.

I called a surprise special meeting with the entire church during the Wednesday evening service and talked with our people about the whole matter. I reminded them that we had voted to remove the tree and now it was gone. I also reminded them that the attitude of our people towards one another about the matter was wrong. I told them at the end of the meeting that the tree was gone, the matter was closed, and I did not want to hear another word about the situation.

Several people apologized to me at the conclusion of the meeting, asking forgiveness for their wrong attitudes and the things they had said. The situation was defused and we moved past it quickly.

As pastor you must live leadership in front of your people. It must be done in private as well as in public. You must show them where they need to go, tell them what must be done to get there, and lead to the ultimate destination.

A great book that can be a tremendous help to you is <u>Lead With Confidence</u>. The book expands into many other areas that will help you model good leadership.

Lead With Confidence

By Dr. Roy W. Harris

(Available on Amazon.com in paperback and Kindle additions.)

The book provides a practical approach to leadership that rookie and veteran leaders alike can use every day in the office.

The book deals with *decision making, second guessing past decisions, relationship building, leadership discernment, receiving and giving criticism, communication, delegating responsibility, admonishing or disciplining, conducting business meetings, and more.*

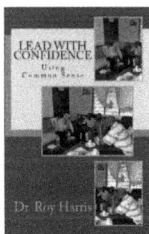

The book is actually two books in one. The original 12 chapters on leadership are complemented by a Study Guide to be used as an aid, helping the reader better grasp the principles found in the book. The Study Guide is divided into 12 sections and is conveniently located between chapters.

Develop a Good Work Ethic

Ecclesiastes 9:10; *Whatever your hand finds to do, do it with your might, for there is no work or thought or knowledge or wisdom in Sheol, to which you are going.* (ESV)

Proverbs 13:4; *The soul of the sluggard craves and gets nothing, while the soul of the diligent is richly supplied.*

Proverbs 12:24; *The hand of the diligent will rule, while the slothful will be put to forced labor.*

Philippians 4:13; *I can do all things through him who strengthens me.*

Proverbs 14:23; *In all toil there is profit, but mere talk tends only to poverty.*

1 Corinthians 10:31; *So, whether you eat or drink, or whatever you do, do all to the glory of God.*

A deacon was asked what kind of pastor he wanted for his church. He responded by saying *I don't want either a workaholic pastor or a lazy pastor. Unfortunately, our last two pastors have been lazy.*

A boy's father was raised during the Great Depression, and he realized the benefits and discipline of hard work. He did not want his son to grow up 'soft.' When the boy was sixteen, his father sent him to work with Martin Brock, a farmer who was over sixty years of age. Martin had agreed to clear some land for a new golf course this young man's father was building in early June in central Minnesota. The boy reported to work on a sweltering day in blue jeans, work boots and a t-shirt.

Martin was a little thin man dressed in dark green work clothes. The sweat dripping from his forehead did not seem to bother him. He removed a greasy-looking green baseball cap, wiped his forehead, and flipped it back on his bald head. In a broken Dutch accent, he said, *We work hard; we take 15-minute breaks twice a day, one at ten and one at three. We eat lunch in thirty minutes, and then work hard again. Pick up that ax and follow me.*

He turned around and was in the woods before the boy could reach the ax near a tree stump. The boy followed the thumping sounds of chopping. When the boy reached him, Martin said, *Like this*.

He grabbed a small tree with his strong left hand, and with one powerful blow, chopped it near the root with his right. He tossed the tree aside. Then, he moved to another and repeated the routine, again and again. The boy probably stood there half a minute, watching him in awe. He moved quickly, yet gracefully. He was skinny, but strong.

Suddenly, Martin stopped and turned to gaze at the boy. *Why aren't you working? Work!* Immediately he returned to his chronic motion of chopping.

You will never guess what happened 2 hours later...... I will tell you at the end of this chapter.

I remember reading an article by Erin Shreiner that sparked my thinking. Schreiner listed some characteristics that are usually present in those who have a good work ethic. I want to expand on those characteristics below.

While some individuals try to get by with doing as little work as possible, others give it their all every day. People who possess a strong work ethic hold to certain principles that guide their work behavior. These principles lead them to consistently produce high quality work while staying on track without the prodding or exhortation of others.

Characteristics of a Good Work Ethic

1. One must be reliable.

Reliability is an important characteristic of a pastor's good work ethic. If pastors have a good work ethic and say they are going to be at a certain place at a certain time, they will be there. They believe and practice punctuality.

Pastors with strong work ethics want to be dependable, showing that they are people who can be counted on to get things done. They place high value on showing they are dependable by consistently being reliable and performing.

2. One must be dedicated.

Pastors with a good work ethic are dedicated to their ministries and will do anything they can to ensure that their ministries do well. Often, this dedication leads them to change churches less frequently. They become committed to their positions and are not eager to abandon these posts.

Dedicated pastors often put in extra hours, making it easy for others to see that they are pastors who go above and beyond what is minimally required. They dedicate themselves to their positions.

3. One must be productive.

Pastors with good work ethics are often highly productive. They work at a consistent pace and get things done. They get large amounts of work done more quickly than others who lack their work ethic. They will not quit until they have completed the tasks that need to be done.

4. One must be able to cooperate.

Cooperation is absolutely necessary in the pastoral ministry. Pastors with strong work ethics understand this well. Pastors with strong work ethics often put extensive amounts of effort into working well with others because they recognize the usefulness of cooperation and teamwork. A dedicated work ethic sometimes requires pastors to work with people with whom they may not enjoy working.

5. One must possess good character.

Pastors with good work ethics often possess strong character as well. This is developed more fully in another chapter but is also worth addressing here.

Pastors with good character are self-disciplined, pushing themselves to complete ministry tasks instead of requiring others to step in and complete their work.

They are honest and trustworthy. They view these traits as befitting high-quality pastors they want to become. Pastors demonstrate their strong character by living these positive traits daily, which makes them rise above many other professions in the world.

Back to our story...

A boy's father was raised during the Great Depression and realized the benefits and discipline of hard work. He did not want his son to grow up 'soft.'

When the boy was sixteen, his father sent him to work with Martin Brock, a farmer who was over sixty years of age. Martin had agreed to clear some land for a new golf course this young man's father was building in early June in central Minnesota. The boy reported to work on a sweltering day in blue jeans, work boots and a t-shirt.

Martin was a little thin man dressed in dark green work clothes, and the sweat that was dripping from his forehead did not seem to bother him. He removed a greasy-looking green baseball cap, wiped his forehead, and flipped it back on his bald head.

In a broken Dutch accent, he said, *We work hard; we take 15-minute breaks twice a day, one at ten and one at three. We eat lunch in thirty minutes and then work hard again. Pick up that ax and follow me.*

He turned around and was in the woods before the boy could reach the ax near a tree stump. The boy followed the thumping sounds of chopping. When the boy reached him, Martin said, *Like this.*

He grabbed a small tree with his strong left hand and with one powerful blow, chopped it near the root with his right. He tossed the tree aside. Then, he moved to another and repeated the routine, again and again. The boy probably stood there a half a minute, watching him in awe. He moved quickly, yet gracefully. He was skinny but strong.

Suddenly, Martin stopped and turned to gaze at the boy: *Why aren't you working? Work!* Immediately, he returned to his chronic motion of chopping.

Two hours later, completely exhausted, the boy slumped to the ground. He remembers thinking, *Thank God it's ten a.m.!* Martin sat on a log near the boy and sipped black, hot coffee from the metal cap of his Thermos.

He stared at the boy, then winked and said, *I thought you were strong football player. You not in good shape at all. I'm old man; you not keep up vid me?* The boy did not reply; he just shook his head, wondering if he could make it until noon.

Well, the boy made it until noon and the end of the day. Martin got him in shape and when the boy returned to school that fall, he was tough as nails. No, make that as tough as Martin. That was the most difficult and yet the greatest, summer of the boy's life.

The boy learned from Martin, not only the value of hard work in teaching responsibility, accountability and commitment, but also the good feeling of accomplishment and healthy self-esteem that hard work delivers.

A good work ethic will usher pastors towards success, but a bad work ethic will eventually sweep them away to irrelevancy. Hard work pays huge dividends.

Be *reliable, dedicated, productive, cooperative and a pastor with good character.* Discipline yourself and make yourself do what needs to be done. Do what you say you will do. Be where you say you will be. Get up every day and go to work.

Develop a good work ethic early. If you do, you will set a pattern in place that will help you the rest of your life.

Share Your Vision

A deacon said, *Our church has so much possibility; I want to hear what we will do to make a difference in our community and the world.*

Proverbs 29:18 states, *Where there is no prophetic vision the people are discouraged, but blessed is he who keeps the law.* (ESV)

Pastors and vision go hand in hand. Churches must have vision. What is vision?

Vision is a picture or idea you have in your mind of yourself and your church, and what you hope will happen. Pastors with clear vision will develop a sense of purpose and direction. Their vision will help guide their churches in pursuing their hopes, dreams, and goals resulting in strong belief and confidence in the pastor and the direction the church is heading.

It started like many evenings with mom at home and Jimmy playing after dinner. Jimmy's parents were busy with the evening's tasks and did not notice the time.

The light from the bright full moon began to seep through the windows. Mom glanced at the clock and said, *Jimmy, it's time to go to bed. Go up now and I'll come and settle you later.* Jimmy usually required additional urging from his parents, but tonight he immediately went straight upstairs to his room.

Jimmy's mother came up to check on him an hour or so later. To her astonishment, she found her son staring quietly out of his window at the moonlit sky.

What are you doing, Jimmy? she inquired.

I'm looking at the moon, Mommy.

Then she said, *Well, it's time to go to bed now.*

Jimmy was reluctant to settle into bed. What he said to his mother that night was almost unbelievable and probably impossible. I will tell you at the end of the chapter what Jimmy said.

Dr. Ronnie Floyd is a well-known pastor, writer, and conference speaker who has impacted thousands of pastors nationwide and on the international stage. He is certainly a man who knows much about vision and effective ways of casting vision, and he has a track record to prove it.

Below are some of Dr. Floyd's helpful suggestions that I have noted and expanded on along with what I have learned through personal experience.

Effectively Cast Your Vision

There is a great deal of material available on how to develop vision and formulate it into a vision statement. I will not take time to expand on it here. A little research will reveal that there is a plethora of resources to guide pastors in developing vision for their churches.

Vision casting by pastors can sometimes be intimidating, and many approach it with fear and trembling. It does not have to be that way. If pastors are going to enjoy success in the ministry, they must have vision and learn to effectively pass it along to their people.

The bigger the vision, the more important it is to involve a variety of people from different age groups, backgrounds and skills. Working with others in discerning the Lord's will can be rewarding and can lend confidence and credibility to the vision when it is communicated later to the rest of the congregation.

Below are a few helpful things to remember and to use as a guide in casting vision.

1. Write down the vision. Writing down the vision is always good. Once it is written down with specifics, it will be much easier to prepare an approach and communicate it. As the communicator, you must be clear about your understanding of it. This is also why writing down the vision is imperative. This written documentation is what you will return to again and again.

2. Clearly cast the vision. The most important thing a leader can do in casting a vision is to be clear. When God has given you a vision, share it with others clearly.

When the vision is clear to you, you are more able to clearly communicate it to others. Through a meticulous process, you learn how to communicate the vision clearly. Whether you are communicating the vision of the church or the vision for a new initiative, ensure you do so with absolute clarity.

It is not about how much you share, but you must share enough for people to have complete clarity or understanding.

3.　*Make the vision believable.* Having a believable vision means that your vision is real and tangible. Sharing a believable vision is not using language that people do not understand or trying to impress them with a huge amount of information. People must be able to touch, feel, and personally become engaged with the vision.

Be careful not to over-spiritualize the vision. We have to know God wants us to do it. We cannot always spiritualize an initiative and have it received by the people, but we must communicate the vision in a believable and tangible manner.

4.　*Keep the vision simple.* If you want people to grasp your vision, keep it simple. Making it too complex absolutely destroys the ability to understand and embrace a vision. Detail is important, but limit how much detail you share; otherwise, people may get lost in your vision. People must grasp the vision, or they probably will not support it.

Ensure that you cast your vision in a simple manner if you want the participation, verbal support and financial support of your congregation. Less is more in today's world. This is especially true when we cast a vision. It needs to be concise, brief and free from too many details. You should go deep enough to comprehend the details, so you know you understand the vision. However, when you cast it before others, they need to know the work is already done.

You need to be on top of it, but remember, you are breaking it down so others can grasp it and so they will be able to communicate it to still others. Share your vision in a simple way, with enough information for the people to have complete understanding of where you want to take them and what you hope to do.

5. *Support the vision biblically.* Show how your vision will reach others for Christ and how it will make disciples. Reinforce that vision with God's Word. This is also a good way for you to test your vision and make sure it is in line and in tune with the Word of God. People will usually embrace the vision when they see how it is tied to God's Word.

6. *Be creative in the way you share the vision.* Ask the Lord to guide your thinking on how best to present your vision. My practice was to

casually share one-on-one with as many key people as I could. I also shared with small groups. I tried to do my best to make sure the majority of my congregations knew as much as possible before I ever presented the vision collectively to the entire congregation.

I never presented my vision or any item that needed the approval and support of my people unless I was convinced that I would receive it. Every item that I presented in each of my churches was usually unanimously approved and supported.

7.   *Use technology to put an image and face on your vision.* Human beings are visual. They remember more of what they see than what they hear. PowerPoint, printed handouts, etc. help people better understand the vision that is being cast.

Never have so many opportunities existed to get people excited about a vision being cast. Brainstorming with your leadership team about all the visual ways you can share the vision is a great idea. People love to see where you want them to go. Technology is a friend to casting vision. Show them!

8.   *Be enthusiastic when casting the vision.*

The expression, *Enthusiasm breed's enthusiasm* is certainly true. If you want your people to be excited about the vision, then you must be excited about your vision first. Passionate enthusiasm always attracts people and inspires them. You must be passionate about your vision if you hope to convince your people to follow it. You must be excited and enthusiastic about what God is doing and what He is calling you to do!

Back to our story…

It started like many evenings with Jimmy playing after dinner. Jimmy's parents were busy with the evening's tasks and did not notice the time.

The light from the bright full moon began to seep through the windows. Mom glanced at the clock and said, *Jimmy, it's time to go to bed. Go up now and I'll come and settle you later.*

Jimmy usually required additional urging from his parents, but tonight he immediately went straight upstairs to his room. Jimmy's mother came up to check on him an hour or so later. To her astonishment, she found her son staring quietly out of his window at the moonlit sky.

What are you doing, Jimmy? she inquired.

I'm looking at the moon, Mommy.

—

Then she said, *Well, it's time to go to bed now.*

Jimmy was reluctant to settle into bed. What he said to his mother that night was almost unbelievable and probably impossible.

Mommy, you know one day I'm going to walk on the moon.

Who could have known that the boy in whom that dream was planted that night would survive a near fatal motorcycle crash which broke almost every bone in his body? The boy's name is James Irwin, and 32 years later he stepped off a lunar module onto the moon's surface. He then took his first steps and walked on the moon, just one of the 12 representatives of humanity to do so.

A compelling vision moves the people to action. As a servant-leader, you are God's instrument to rally the people to a better future. You are there to lead them into a future where they would not go on their own.

You must:
- *Clearly cast your vision.*
- *Make your vision believable.*
- *Keep your vision simple.*
- *Support your vision biblically.*
- *Be creative in the way you share your*

vision.

• *Use technology to put an image and face on your vision.*

• *Be enthusiastic when casting your vision.*

As the communicator of the vision, do your very best to be strong, believable and capable of moving people into enthusiastically owning the vision. If the vision is going to capture your people's imagination and hearts and move them into committing personally and enthusiastically, then the vision must be compelling.

Leadership is a privilege, because you are able to cast your vision to others. Handle what you have been entrusted well. You have the privilege of taking them where you believe God wants them to go. Share your vision!

Baptize New Christians

I was in the early days of my first pastorate in Ahoskie, North Carolina and excited about the baptisms that would take place after our worship service later that morning. It was wintertime, and I walked across the street from the parsonage to turn on the heat in the sanctuary and double check the baptistery.

To my horror, the baptistery heater had gone out and the baptistery water was ice cold. Six people were scheduled for baptism that morning, and I found myself in quite a difficult situation.

You'll never guess what happened that Sunday morning. I will finish the story at the end of the chapter.

I remember the Sunday afternoon when my pastor Reverend Dalton Heath baptized me. It was such a special time and a day I will never forget. I remember it like it was yesterday. The same is true for most people when they follow the Lord's command and are baptized.

An important responsibility of the pastor is to baptize new converts. These converts will range in age from young children to senior adults. Each one is important, and there are some basic actions that might be helpful to remember.

1. Talk with baptism candidates before scheduling baptisms. There are number of reasons for this. You should make sure candidates have accepted Christ and have assurance of their salvation. You should also make sure they understand what baptism represents, they know why they are going to be baptized and they know exactly what they are doing.

2. Describe in detail what will happen during the baptism. This is especially important when baptizing children, but important for all who will be baptized. I often do a small demonstration with them ahead of time, showing how they should hold their hands, how I will hold my hands, how I will place them under the water, etc. I also share the words I will say just before placing them under the water.

3. Schedule the baptism at least two weeks in advance. Work with the candidates to see what will work best for their schedules, your schedule and the church calendar. This should be discussed in the early meeting and finalized after everyone involved has time to look at schedules.

One of the main reasons for scheduling the baptism at least a couple of weeks in the future is to provide candidates the opportunity to invite family and friends to be present. This provides a perfect way of bringing unsaved family and friends into God's house to sit under the preaching of God's Word.

4. Schedule baptisms on Sunday mornings. I have found that Sunday mornings have worked best for me. Typically, the largest weekly crowd will be present on Sunday morning. Baptisms encourage the church family, and more of them will be present on Sunday mornings. Nothing does more for the morale of churches than folks getting saved and baptized. It is also more likely that family and friends of baptism candidates will come on Sunday mornings.

5. Make sure the baptistery is clean, filled, heated and ready for baptismal services. Someone should be delegated this responsibility. But in the end, the pastor is responsible and must make sure this is done.

6. Make sure you have private changing rooms for men and women. Candidates will want to change into dry clothes after the baptism service is over.

7. Secure others ahead of time to assist the candidates before, during and after the baptism - a lady to help ladies and girls and a man to help men and boys. They will help the candidates navigate the steps when entering and leaving the baptistery. They will help them with towels to dry themselves off and make sure they have privacy when changing clothes.

8. Wear chest waders. I purchased a pair of black waders and wore a black minister's robe over them. This kept me dry so I could change quickly and still make it to the lobby to greet our guests and church family after the service.

9. Plan wisely the order in which to baptize candidates.

- Try to baptize children first in the order. They tend to be more anxious and sometimes even a little afraid.

- Baptize married couples next - wives first,

and then their husbands.

- If there are no couples, then ladies should be baptized first, followed by the men.

10. Make sure you can be heard from the baptistery. We had a drop-down microphone in the baptistery located just above my head in one church that I pastored. I used a lapel mike in another church. It is important that the congregation hears what is being said and sees what is taking place in the baptistery.

11. Explain what baptism is, what it represents and why Christians should be baptized.

12. Share a brief testimony about each person as they are about to be baptized. Recount details of their salvation experience and their relationship with the church.

13. Develop your own style and approach when placing people under the water. Develop your own words and routine. I usually have the person hold their nose with their right hand. I grasp their right forearm with my right hand and ask them to grasp my right forearm with their left hand. I hold on to them and they hold on to me. I raise my left hand towards heaven. I am now set to place them under the water.

14. *Baptize in the name of the Father, the Son and the Holy Ghost.* I developed what I would say at this point in my first church many years ago and have repeated it in all the churches I have pastored. I raise my left hand and say, *In accordance with the command of our Lord and Savior Jesus Christ, I baptize this my (brother or sister), in the name of the Father, the Son and the Holy Ghost, Amen.*

I place my left hand in the middle of the person's back and place him or her under the water. I have already told them to please keep their legs straight, lean back and let me do all the work. I watch and make sure I get their heads completely under the water.

15. *Help each person back to the steps and make sure they are safely in the hands of those assisting you.*

16. *Turn to the congregation and give some final words.* I always ask the congregation to pray for

those who were just baptized as they begin their new life in Christ. I always communicate with my worship leader and ask him to be prepared to lead the congregation in some songs while waiting for me to come into the baptistery and also afterwards to give me time to make a quick change so I can greet the congregation in the lobby as they are leaving.

17. *Prepare a baptism certificate for each person.* This does not have to be done on the day of the baptism, but is should be done soon after.

Ministering to the Sick

You're not doing your job, the caller said. *You're not being a good pastor*. What was the problem? A parishioner had surgery in the hospital and the pastor was not present. I will give more details and finish the story at the end of the chapter.

Ministering to the sick is an important part of a pastor's responsibilities. He must take it seriously! There are a number of things that might be helpful for pastors to remember about ministering to the sick.

A Good Principle to Follow

I had the privilege of serving on the administration at Welch College as Dean of Students. One of my primary responsibilities was student discipline. I was *the sheriff* so to speak, and it was up to me to make sure the rules of the college were enforced and obeyed.

I developed a principle during those days that has served me well. Simply put: *Any exception to a rule becomes the new rule.* In other words, if I made an exception for one student, then I would have to make that same exception for any other students with a similar situation.

I knew that students talked among themselves and the decisions I made would make their way through the student body. Mental notes from past decisions would be reviewed and compared by students. It would not take long for apparent inconsistencies and seemingly special treatment to rise to the top level of student discussions.

Following this principle helped me greatly in the pastorate, and I believe it can help you also. Consistency in ministry is important, and consistency in ministering to the sick is paramount.

Please remember that what you do in one situation will become your expected behavior by your congregation in any and all similar situations from that moment on. Develop behavior patterns for situations like:

- When will I be present for surgeries?
- How often should I visit my parishioners in the hospital?
- Should I be present for outpatient surgeries?

- Should I rush to the emergency room when parishioners are transported?
- What are the dos and don'ts of hospital visitation?
- Should I visit my congregation after they leave the hospital and return home?

Developing behavior patterns and trying to stick to them will help you stay consistent in the way you treat each parishioner.

Helpful Surgery Guidelines

Below are a few suggestions that might be helpful in developing some personal guidelines when your parishioners are scheduled for surgery.

1. Should I be present for the surgery? Your people will have a variety of surgeries at different locations. Some surgeries will require spending time in the hospital and others may be outpatient surgery at a clinic or similar medical facility.

I developed a principle that has served me well in all four of my full-time pastorates. My guiding principle is: *If the surgery requires my parishioner to be placed under anesthesia, then I attend the surgery.* Anesthetists always warn patients before surgery that there are serious risks any time a person undergoes anesthesia. There is something reassuring to people when their pastor is there, and one of the last things that happens before being put under is hearing his prayer for God's protection and a successful outcome for their surgery.

Be careful about trying to be at every medical procedure your people undergo. You will spend time you do not have in an impossible task with endless medical procedures. You will also be inconsistent with your people, because every person and every surgery is different. The whole matter can contribute to ministry burnout.

2. I'm planning to be at the surgery. What are some things I need to remember? There are several things you may want to keep in mind that have helped me through the years.

• *Touch base with the family the evening before the scheduled surgery to confirm that it is still on.* Find out the location where they are to report at the hospital. You will learn quickly where to go for surgeries at your local hospital(s). You will also learn quickly where the family surgery waiting area is.

- *Ask them to please let you know if, for some reason, the surgery is cancelled or the schedule has changed.* I have shown up at the hospital a few times early in the morning, only to discover the patient and/or family are not there and the surgery had been postponed or rescheduled for later in the day. Families do not automatically remember to call the pastor to let him know that the schedule has changed.

- *Arrive an hour early for the scheduled surgery.* Patients are normally prepped and sometimes taken down to the surgery holding area before the scheduled surgery time. It is much better to be thirty minutes early than five minutes late.

- *Always ask to have prayer with the patient.* I usually say something like, *Would you mind if we have a word of prayer to ask the Lord to be with you and watch over you during your surgery?* I have yet to have anyone turn me down.

- *Be conscious of the family and their need to be close to the patient.* I generally step back after having prayer and let the family members surround their loved one and say their goodbyes. This time can be very emotional for the family and the patient.

• *Determine how long you will stay.* There are basically two practices pastors follow when deciding how long to stay during surgeries. Either approach is okay. One approach is to have prayer with the patient and check back later in the day. The other is to have prayer with the patient and remain with the family during the surgery.

My personal approach is to stay with the family during the surgery until they receive word that the surgery is over and they hear the report from the surgeon. The report might be in person or by phone. The key for me is knowing the patient is out of surgery and doing fine. Then I excuse myself, shift gears and head out to continue my day.

I developed this approach early in my ministry. I wanted my people to know that I would be there for them. There is special comfort in having your pastor there during this time of uncertainty.

Whichever approach you adopt, be consistent. Do not stay with one family during surgery and not another. Word will get out quickly among your people, and it may appear that you think more of some families than others. Do not change your approach in midstream. Wait until you begin pastoring another church before making the change.

3. The surgery is over. Now what? Return to the hospital the next day to check on the patient. From that point on, follow your regular hospital visitation routine.

4. What about outpatient surgery at a surgery center or clinic? Follow the same guidelines as mentioned in hospital surgeries above.

Helpful Hospital Visitation Guidelines

Hospital visitation is an important part of pastoral duties. You must be careful to take care of yourself, look out for the patient's health and not spend too much time visiting hospitals. There are some things I learned that helped me keep balanced and may be helpful to you also.

1. How often should I visit my parishioners in the hospital? This really depends on the seriousness of the illness. A general rule that I follow is to visit patients every other day. I call them on the days I do not visit the hospital. It is amazing what a phone call can accomplish. The fact that you thought of the patient and took time to call will mean a lot to most people.

If you try to visit each day, it will hinder your other duties and responsibilities and interrupt your primary responsibility of preparing to preach to your people. Other things you should be doing become secondary and may be left undone or half done.

Patients in life and death situations are a bit different and should be visited daily. I have made two visits in one day on a few occasions. If the person is not expected to live, I keep in close touch with the family. Each situation will be different, but God's Holy Spirit will help you. Depend on Him!

2. *What are some things I should remember when visiting the hospital?* There are a few basic things I try to do each time I visit the hospital.

- *Visit the hospital chaplain's office and get to know the chaplain.* Chaplain office personnel will share with you the clergy visitation dos and don'ts.
- *The hospital may require a clergy security badge.* The chaplain's office should be able to help you with the process. I kept my badge in the primary vehicle I used for my ministry work. Place it in the console or glove box. You will occasionally decide to make an unplanned hospital visit while out of the office. Keeping your badge in your vehicle will save a

trip back to the office or to your home. It will also remove the possibility of just plain forgetting to take the badge with you.

• *Take advantage of clergy parking when available.* Some hospitals provide designated clergy parking, usually strategically located to save time for ministers, recognizing that they visit the hospital on a regular basis and several times more than the average person.

• *Always knock before entering a patient's room.* Entering unannounced could result in embarrassment for the patient as well as the minister.

• *Use hand sanitizer.* Always wash your hands or use hand sanitizer before entering patients' rooms. I used to always stop by the restroom and wash my hands before entering patients' rooms. Hand sanitizer is a wonderful invention. Dispensers are strategically located in many public buildings and easily accessible. Use soap and water if hand sanitizer is not available.

Hospital patients are especially vulnerable to germs and infection. Their resistance is usually low and the less exposure, the better for them. I always wash my hands using a dispenser near the patient's room before entering. I feel more at ease shaking hands with others in the room, along with the patient. I also wash my hands using a dispenser after leaving the patient's room. You cannot be too safe, so if your instinct is to wash your hands, then wash your hands.

- *Keep your visit brief.* Ten to fifteen minutes is adequate time to greet everyone in the room, enquire about the patient's condition and progress, and pray. Do not overstay! The patient needs rest, and many times the family will feel that they must entertain you. Minister to the patient and family, and then move on.

- *Pray with the patient.* Prayer can be a great comfort to patients and their families. Always ask if you may have prayer. Be perceptive and kind. The Holy Spirit will guide you in when and how to pray.

Pray for the patient by name. Call the individual by the name you normally use in conversation. It is also appropriate to use *brother* or *sister* so and so. Pray specifically for the patient's needs. Pray also for the family members, especially the primary caregiver.

As you leave, remind them to please let you know if they need you. Also, let them know that you will touch base later. Be careful about promising to stop by or contact them the next day. Something unexpected could come up and create a conflict.

  • *There are a few miscellaneous things that will be helpful to remember.*

    i. Always carry breath mints and use them!

    ii. Dress appropriately and look like the pastor your people will be glad to see and proud to introduce to others.

    iii. Stop by the hospital the next day after surgery if possible.

    iv. Call on the days you do not visit the hospital to check on the patient. Call before you drive to the hospital and double check to make sure the patient is still there. I have driven to the hospital, only to discover the patient was discharged early. It may save you a wasted trip, car expense and precious time that could be used for something else.

Back to our story...

You're not doing your job, the caller said. *You're not being a good pastor*. What was the problem? A parishioner had surgery in the hospital and the pastor was not present.

One thing I learned early in my ministry was

that some things are not my fault. I developed a practice that served me well in all my churches. Early in my tenure at each church, I had what I fondly liked to call *a family chat.* I would mention a few things about which I wanted my people and me to come to an understanding.

One such thing was being with my people when they needed me. I let them know from the pulpit that I wanted to be there when they had surgeries, death in the family, etc. I also let them know that I was not omniscient like God, nor was I clairvoyant. I shared that I would only know the things about which people informed me. I told them to please not make the test of whether or not the church or I cared about them based on whether I could find out about a surgery or death without a member of their family letting me know.

I publicly said to them: *Please don't accuse me of not caring or not being a good pastor if you didn't let me know about a surgery or death.*

This 'chat' helped me tremendously. There were a few times along the way that I was unaware of situations and church members became upset, but others came to my defense, asking the family, *Did you let Brother Roy know?*

Final Thoughts

Your people need your thoughts, prayers and attention when they are sick. Use common sense when making decisions on how best to minister to them. Following the suggestions mentioned above can provide a framework that may be helpful as you develop guidelines and set patterns for ministering to the sick.

One very important thing to remember: Be consistent in the way you minister to your congregation. This is especially true in ministering to the sick. Your people will know if you are consistent or if you are not. Be there for you people when they need you. Minister to the sick of your congregation.

Visit Your People

I remember reading a story about a young bride who was preparing one of her first meals for her new husband. She had learned from his mother that one of his favorite meals was beef roast.

She took the carefully chosen roast from the refrigerator, proceeded to cut off both ends and placed it in the slow cooker. She added carrots and potatoes and set a timer so it would be ready when they both arrived home from work later in the day.

Her husband, observing his wife's hard work and enjoying the wonderful aroma in the kitchen, sat down to the wonderful meal his wife had prepared. Something had been bothering him all day about the meal. He could hold it in no longer. You will never guess what was bothering him and what he asked his wife. I will tell you the rest of the story at the end of the chapter.

Should pastors visit their congregations? There is much discussion, and there are many differing opinions on the matter. Thomas Rainer is a well-known pastor and the founder and CEO of Church Answers, an online community and resource for church leaders. Prior to founding Church Answers, Rainer served as president and CEO of LifeWay Christian Resources.

Occasionally I have read Rainer's blog and have enjoyed looking at his insight into ministry matters. He set off a small firestorm with his August 31, 2016 blog titled: *Fifteen Reasons Why Your Pastor Should Not Visit*. He received over 400 comments, and many were not favorable. His article was also mentioned and argued against online in other blogs and social media sites. I will not argue either position, but I believe the best approach is found somewhere in the middle. I will share my approach below.

Helpful Hints for Visiting Your People

1.   *Should I visit my people*? Visiting your people is part of the job description. I understood quickly that it was important for me to visit my people. Not visiting your people will result in a

disconnect and hinder your ability to minister to them. Yes, you should and must visit your people!

2.   *When should I visit?* I learned in my first church that trying to visit every family in the church each year was nearly impossible. It took too much time and pulled me away from other things that I needed to be doing. I learned to visit when a visit was needed. How does one know when he should visit? There are a variety of times, and below I have listed a few.

• Visit in times of illness, (more will be said about this later in the chapter.)

• Visit when a loved one has passed away. You may be the one who must share the difficult news of a loved one's tragic passing with the family. It fell my responsibility to do this on several occasions, such as when a brother was murdered and a young lady in her twenties committed suicide.

• Visit the shut-ins. They may be homebound, in an assisted living facility or nursing home. I tried to make it my practice to stop by at least once a month and sometimes more, depending on the events that arose with them. I set aside one day a month in my schedule to stop by and visit with them.

• Visit when you sense discouragement. You may sense discouragement when observing people as they attend church services. You may hear about it from a friend or family member. The Holy Spirit may simply bring them to mind and impress you to go by for a visit.

• Visit when bad news is received. Visit when the individual or a family member receives a bad report from the doctor. Diagnosis of a life-changing disease can be devastating to your church members. They need a compassionate heart, a kind word and the presence of their pastor.

• Visit when someone loses his or her job. Use common sense. Be careful about entering into situations that could create problems for you. Do not rush in until you know a few details. It could be embarrassing for the church member, and you do not want to put him or her in an awkward position. The change may involve downsizing, a company closing or moving, etc.

• Visit when there seems to be a problem. Be careful! Go to them privately if you sense they have a problem with you, their pastor. Be sure someone else is present if it involves a lady. Also, go talk with them if you have heard there may be a problem between them and other individuals in the church.

Things to remember when visiting your people:

1. *Be consistent*. Set your church member visiting parameters and follow them. Be careful about visiting one family and failing to visit another when both have basic the same circumstances. Please believe me, your people will talk among themselves and compare notes. You do not want them to feel that others are more important to you than they seem to be.

2. *Make an appointment.* I made the mistake early in my ministry of stopping by unannounced a couple of times. The people were not expecting me, and it placed both of us in an awkward situation. Set a time

that is convenient for both parties. This is not an absolute. Some people want you to drop by any time. You may also see someone out in the yard and pull in and visit with them for a few minutes without getting out of your car.

3. *Be on time!* Be there by the appointed time. I try to be a few minutes early. Do not be too early or one minute late.

4. *Call if you will be late or you need to reschedule.* Unforeseen circumstances arise from time to time that may cause you to be late. Call *before* the scheduled time and as soon as possible to let others know that you will be late or that you need to reschedule. Explain and give enough details to help them understand your situation.

5. *Limit your visit to about 30 minutes.* Do not wear out your welcome. You can normally do what needs to be done within that time frame. Leave your members desiring you to stay longer rather than wondering if you are ever going to leave. There will be times when the situation will warrant a longer visit. Your pastoral instinct led by the Holy Spirit will guide

you.

6. *Do not visit married ladies when their husbands are not present or teenagers when their parents are not home.* That should go without saying, but there it is; I just said it.

7. *Take your wife with you when visiting widows.* I make a practice of never being alone with a lady, regardless of how old or young she is. That would be a good practice for you to consider also.

8. *Be careful about visiting your people at work.* By and large, this is not a good practice. It might create problems between your church members and their supervisors. You will not be able to accomplish much in that type setting.

There are exceptions to this policy. I have had business owners who loved for me to stop by when I was near their places of business. I always waited for their invitation before making my first visit and only stayed a few minutes each time.

9. *Do not become too close to one family in the church.* Your church members will notice your

spending a great deal of time with one family.

Back to our story...

She took the roast from the refrigerator, proceeded to cut off both ends and placed it in the slow cooker. Adding carrots and potatoes, she set a timer so it would be ready when they both arrived home from work later in the day.

Her husband, observing his wife's hard work and enjoying the aroma from the kitchen, sat down to the wonderful meal his wife had prepared. Something had been bothering him all day about the meal. He could hold it in no longer. *Honey, why do you cut off both ends of the roast before you place it in the cooker?* he asked.

My mother always cut off the ends before cooking a roast, she replied.

Do you know why she did it? he questioned.

No, but I'm going to ask her, the wife replied.

She called her mother and asked her why she always cut the end off the roasts. Her mother did not know either, only that her mother, the lady's grandmother, had done it that way. The lady decided to ask her grandmother. She called her and asked,

Grandmother, why did you always cut the ends of your roasts when Mom was growing up?

Well honey, it was because the roasts were usually bigger than my cooking pans, and that was the only way I could make them fit.

We should understand the value and importance of visiting our people. We should also know our limitations and determine what works for us. Knowing what needs to be done, how best to go about it and the basics that will make visitation practical, effective and successful are essential.

We learn from others and we learn by experience. Be there when your people need you. Your compassionate heart, kind words and pastor's face are important to your people. All members should feel that they are personally important to you, their pastor.

Minister in Times of Loss

The death of a church member is an important time in the life of a church. The church staff should develop a protocol for how they will handle the loss of church members. This should include the role the congregation will play.

The size of the church staff will dictate how loss will be handled. Many times, the main responsibility will fall to the pastor, especially in smaller churches.

I developed a mental checklist that has helped me along the way. Situations are different, but a few things remain constant throughout times of loss.

1.   Contact should be made with the family suffering the loss as soon as possible. I usually drop what I am doing, if possible, and go directly to the family.

2. I do not ask the family a lot of questions about the death. I wait for them to share whatever they would like for me to know.

3. Most churches have an individual or a committee who plans and delivers meals to the family. This will vary with each death. A heads-up should be given to the appropriate person that the death has occurred, but no formal plans should be made until more details about the family's plans are known.

4. The same is true with flowers. The appropriate person who orders flowers should be notified. A note of caution: You and your leadership should develop a policy on when flowers should be sent from the church. This will help the church be consistent and head off potential problems and hurt feelings.

5. I ask a family member to give me a call when they finalize the funeral arrangements. The church should be informed as soon as possible when arrangements are finalized and known. This is much easier with email and social media options.

6.   Many times, you will be asked to take part in the funeral service. Most of the time, you will play an active part in helping the family plan the service. I usually set a time to meet with the family to find out what they would like included in the service. I ask these basic questions:

- Are there any other ministers they want to have part in the service? If so, what would they like them to do?

- Are there any family members or friends who they would like to speak or have part in the service?

- Are there special scriptures they would like to have read?

- Are there any songs they would like to have sung? If so, who would they like to sing them?

- Do they want the obituary read?

Families will usually leave the final order of service up to you. The important thing to remember is to include all the things the family wants and balance them in an organized fashion.

I print copies of the Order of Service (2 to an 8 ½ X 11 inch sheet and cut them in half into 5 ½ by 8 ½ inch sheets.) I print enough for each person on the program, including extras for funeral home personnel. I pass these along before the service.

Sample Order of Service

(Actual Order of Service that I used)

Mr. William Thompson Memorial Service

Order of Service

Prelude	
Special Music	**Mrs. Kristie Sargent**
Personal Remarks	**Mr. Andrew Thompson**
Congregational Hymn	**"Amazing Grace"**
Personal Remarks	**Mr. Jimmy Thompson**
Special Music	**Mrs. Kristie Sargent**
Funeral Sermon	**Rev. Roy W. Harris**
Postlude	

7. An important thing to remember is that the church staff and church family must show their love and concern for families who lose loved ones. They must look for ways to do this and go the extra mile in this great time of loss and need.

Be Transparent

A deacon was asked about how transparent his pastors had been, and he responded by saying, *Every pastor that I have had has been open and transparent about the church and the direction we are headed. It sure has made our church healthier.*

I was 20 years old, and our country was at war in the country of Vietnam. I was called to serve in the United States Army and went off to basic training to learn how to become a soldier.

I had earned a weekend pass and was allowed to spend the weekend away from the Army base at a friend's house near the end of my training. My friend heated his family's home with firewood. I helped him cut down a big tree, and we cut it into smaller pieces that could be easily burned. We finished cutting the wood and began loading it into a wagon. He threw pieces down a small hill to me and I loaded them into the wagon.

I turned with my arms full of firewood towards the wagon just as he threw a large piece of wood down the hill. The piece flipped end over end picking up speed and hit me on my shin just below my knee. I fell to the ground in agony and pain. You will never guess what happened to my leg. I will tell you at the end of the chapter.

Paul addressed the complaint that he had not been open and honest with the church at Corinth in the body of his second letter to the Corinthians. Even though he promised to visit Corinth again, Paul had backed out twice. Was Paul insincere or speaking out of both sides of his mouth? Was he maneuvering to get his way behind others' backs?

Paul addressed those questions in 2 Corinthians 1:12-14. He was proud that his behavior among the Corinthians had been transparent at all times. His actions were not the machinations of what he calls *fleshly wisdom* in 2 Corinthians 1:12. He did not cancel his visits to gain an advantage for himself or to save face, but because he did not want to shame or rebuke the Corinthians again. He delayed returning to Corinth in the hope that, when he did come, he could bring joy rather than recrimination and reproof (2 Corinthians 1:23-24).

Though Paul's integrity had been questioned, he knew that, because of his history of transparency with the Corinthians, they would continue to trust him. *We have behaved in the world with frankness and godly sincerity*, he reminded them in 2 Corinthians 1:12. Because they had seen him in action, they knew he said what he meant without vacillating (2 Corinthians 1:17-20). Once they knew all the factors he had to consider, he was sure they would understand (2 Corinthians 1:1-13). Evidence of Paul's confidence in their trust is that, even without knowing everything, Paul told them: *You have already understood us in part* 2 Corinthians 1:13.

Are we transparent enough in our work today so that people have a reason to trust us? Every person, company and organization face temptations on a daily basis to hide the truth.

Are we obscuring our motives in order to falsely gain trust from others? Are we making decisions in secret as a way of avoiding accountability or hiding factors to which others would object? Are we pretending to support others in their presence, but speaking critically behind their backs?

Paul's example shows us that these actions are wrong. Whatever brief advantage we might gain is lost in the long term because others learn not to trust us. If others cannot trust us, can God?

This does not mean that we always reveal all the information we have. There are confidences, personal and organizational, that cannot be broken. Not everyone needs to be privy to all information. Sometimes the best answer may be *I can't answer that question because I have a duty of privacy to someone else.* However, we should not use confidentiality as an excuse to gain an edge on others or to portray ourselves in a falsely positive light. If questions surface about our motives, a solid track record of openness and reliability will be the best antidote for misplaced doubts.

Transparency was so important to Paul's work with the Corinthians that he returned to the theme throughout the letter. *We refuse to practice cunning or to falsify Gods word; but by the open statement of the truth we commend ourselves,* he says in 2 Corinthians 4:2. He also says in chapter 6:11, *We have spoken frankly to you Corinthians; our heart is wide open to you.*

What does being transparent really mean? Transparency is a big word that can mean many things. It becomes a lot easier to understand if you think about transparency in relationship to what your congregation wants to know and hear. Here are nine tips to help you become more transparent with your members.

1.   *Be truthful and accurate.* Always tell the truth. If you do not know for sure, then do not substitute only what you have heard.

2.   *Keep the promises you make.* Make sure that whatever you promise, you do. If there are reasons that you are not able to do what you said you would, then make sure others understand why.

3.   *Maintain two-way communication.* Good communication is a two-way channel. Communication loses its value and impact when there is only a one-sided conversation.

4.   *Be timely and responsive.* Responding as quickly as possible to phone calls and emails is not just a suggestion; it should be a requirement. You need to be accessible to your people.

5.   *Admit your mistakes.* Mistakes will

happen. When they do, communicate – do not hide! The sooner you address the issue by solving the problem, the sooner you can move on. Acting quickly to remedy the mistake and taking steps so it will not happen again is the message you want your people to hear.

6. *Share knowledge*. Give your members the information they need.

7. *Inform your congregation about changes.* You will gain their trust and foster greater relationships if you keep them up to date on good or bad changes happening within your church.

8. *Listen to your people.* Your people will be encouraged when they know that someone is listening to them and trying to resolve issues.

9. *Thank your people*. One way to create a positive environment is always to say *thank you*. Kindness and gratitude will cost you nothing and are sure ways to keep your people with you for the long term.

Though it is not always easy, transparency is

crucial for healthy churches and sustained growth.

Back to our story...

We finished cutting up the wood and began loading it into a wagon. He threw pieces down a small hill to me and I loaded them. I turned with my arms full of firewood towards the wagon just as he threw a large piece of wood down the hill. The piece flipped end over end and hit me just below my knee on my shin. I fell to the ground in agony and pain.

I thought my leg was broken. We pulled up the leg of my trousers and the skin had been scraped almost to the bone. The leg was bleeding, and I was in terrible pain. My friend helped me to my feet and into the cab of his old truck.

I spent the rest of the weekend with my leg elevated. The family wanted me to go to the local hospital, but I refused. I returned to post on Sunday evening and spent the night with my leg elevated, not mentioning a word about what had happened to anyone.

We rose early the next morning for our final two weeks of training. I was determined to finish my training, knowing that if I failed to do so, I would have to start my basic training again from the beginning.

Though I tried as hard as I could, I could not keep up. I was limping badly, and it quickly became obvious to my sergeant that something was wrong. He had called on me on many occasions to help those who were struggling to keep up. He had never seen me needing help.

The sergeant asked me what was wrong with my leg. I pulled up my trouser leg and told him the story of what had happened. He and another soldier helped me to the shade and called an ambulance. They transported me to the post hospital and immediately to the emergency room.

I remember it like yesterday! The doctor looked and my leg and told me that I might lose it. There was a possibility that gangrene may have already begun to set in. He scrubbed out the wound and the left it open to drain. They kept me in the hospital for two days attending to my wound and then put me on light duty for the next week. I was able to ride to and from training each day. I graduated with my class and became a real soldier, proudly serving my country for the next six years - two years active duty, one year active reserve and three years inactive reserve.

What is the application? My leg was badly injured. I should have immediately reported it to my sergeant upon returning to post. Those two extra days could have cost me my leg and possibly my life. I tried to continue training when I was physically unable to do so.

Be transparent with your people. They will sense when you are not and their trust and respect for you will gradually erode. They will also sense when you are being transparent. Even when handling difficult things, they will appreciate, respect and learn to trust you more and more.

What kind of pastor do your people want? They want a pastor who is transparent and open!

Keep A Joyful Attitude

I have been blessed in my ministry to travel to many places, and most of the time the distance requires flying. I try to find ways to entertain myself. One thing I like to do is watch people. I sometimes sit facing them as they pass up and down the airport terminals.

I occasionally put a frown of my face as people pass by and watch their reactions. They tend to look away from me and refuse to acknowledge that am sitting there. I grin at others with a big smile. It is amazing how they react. They often smile back, greet me, and seemingly are pleased for the interaction. What a difference a joyful smile makes!

A deacon describing his pastor said, *Our current pastor is a man of joy. His joy and enthusiasm are contagious. I love him for that!*

Would you like to be the kind of pastor your people want? Become a pastor filled with joy, and your joy and enthusiasm will be contagious with your people. They will love you for that!

When I was a young man, the car I owned had a small electrical problem. I diagnosed the problem and went to a local department store to purchase the part that needed replacing. I returned home, only to discover after connecting the part, that it was not the problem. I determined that a small electrical fuse that only cost a few cents to replace was the problem. I had one in my toolbox and did not need the part I had purchased after all.

I returned the part to the store expecting to receive the money I had paid for it. You will never guess what happened when I returned the part to the store. I will tell you rest of the story at the end of the chapter.

I read an online blog by Fred Bittner, https://www.faithgateway.com, that gave some great insight on joy. It sparked my thinking, and I would like to give some practical suggestions to remember about being a pastor who shows joy in his life and to his people.

1.   *Joy is not an emotion that can be forced, fabricated, or faked*. Psalms 137:1-4 NKJV reads: *By*

the rivers of Babylon, There we sat down, yea, we wept when we remembered Zion. We hung our harps upon the willows in the midst of it. For there those who carried us away captive asked of us a song, and those who plundered us requested mirth, saying, Sing us one of the songs of Zion! How shall we sing the Lord's song in a foreign land?

The children of Israel had been taken captive and were asked to sing songs of joy for their captors. There are times when joy eludes us. This is normal, and we need to understand that we will not always feel joyful. Joy cannot be forced, so do not try to force it.

2.   Joy is not dependent upon our circumstances. Psalms 27:5-6 NIV reads: For in the day of trouble he will keep me safe in his dwelling; he will hide me in the shelter of his sacred tent and set me high upon a rock. Then my head will be exalted above the enemies who surround me; at his sacred tent I will sacrifice with shouts of joy; I will sing and make music to the Lord.

• We can be in difficult situations and yet experience joy. Jesus added to this by saying: Blessed are you when people hate you, when they exclude you and insult you and reject your name as evil, because of the Son of Man. Rejoice in that day and leap for joy, because great is your reward in heaven. For that is how their ancestors treated the prophets* in Luke 6:22-23 NIV.

• Though joy cannot be forced, it can be experienced in difficult situations. James adds to this thought with: *Consider it pure joy, my brothers and sisters, whenever you face trials of many kinds, because you know that the testing of your faith produces perseverance* in James 1:2-3 NIV.

3. *Joy is possible when we feel secure in the Lord.*

• Psalm 4:6:8 NIV reads*: Many, Lord, are asking, who will bring us prosperity? Let the light of your face shine on us. Fill my heart with joy when their grain and new wine abound. In peace I will lie down and sleep, for you alone, Lord, make me dwell in safety.*

• While others link their happiness to prosperity, believers can find joy in the Lord. We can add our voice to David's in Psalm 3:3 and proclaim, *But you, O Lord, are a shield about me, my glory and the lifter of my head.*

4.   *Joy comes when we have a clear direction for our lives.*

- We might also use the word purpose. Psalm 16:11 NIV illustrates this principle: *You make known to me the path of life; you will fill me with joy in your presence, with eternal pleasures at your right hand.*

- Jesus said in Matthew 13:44 NIV.: *The kingdom of heaven is like treasure hidden in a field. When a man found it, he hid it again, and then in his joy went and sold all he had and bought that field.*

- Where is your hidden treasure? What is the path of life that God has for you? Are you seeking the fields for the treasure that God has for you?

5.   *Joy comes when we live in God's presence.*

- It is easy to lose focus on what brings real joy in a world where celebrity, success, and money are glorified. Put simply, victories are good, glory is great, and splendor and majesty are their results, but our joy comes when we spend time in God's presence. Psalm 28:6-8 Psalm 28:6; Jude 1:2-5; and 1 Thessalonians 3:9 are great verses that illustrate this point.

6. *Joy comes when we spend our lives praising God.* This principle may be the easiest one to embrace since church worship is filled with praise.

• Let us establish a Biblical pattern of praise. Below are some verses that remind us of this great truth: *And now my head shall be lifted up above my enemies all around me; Therefore I will offer sacrifices of joy in His tabernacle; I will sing, yes, I will sing praises to the Lord* Psalm 27:6 NKJV. *Clap your hands, all you nations; shout to God with cries of joy. For the Lord Most High is awesome, the great King over all the earth. He subdued nations under us, peoples under our feet* Psalm 47:1-3 NIV. *My lips will shout for joy when I sing praise to you. I whom you have delivered* Psalm 71:23 NIV.

• Singing, clapping, and shouting are all parts of joyful worship. The three scriptures above about joy only scratch the surface of examples of praise. Another example of praise found in Luke 19:36-39 NIV.

7. *Joy comes when we live honest Biblical lives.* Perhaps the idea of honesty does not seem to fit with principles of joy, but let us look at the opposite side.

- Dishonesty leads to guilt and discouragement, while honesty breeds satisfaction and peace. When we add the concept of Biblical honesty, then we discover true joy. Psalm 97:10-12 NIV reads: *Let those who love the Lord hate evil, for he guards the lives of his faithful ones and delivers them from the hand of the wicked. Light shines on the righteous and joy on the upright in heart. Rejoice in the Lord, you who are righteous, and praise his holy name.*

- Read Psalm 119. It adds some important principles about following God and being honest by following the scripture. There is no greater place to live than in the center of God's will. There is no way to be in the center of His will without living according to the word of God. Living according to Biblical principles leads to a joyful life.

- *Joy comes when we continually praise what God has already done.* Psalm 92:4-5 NIV says: *For you make me glad by your deeds, Lord: I sing for joy at what your hands have done. How great are your works, Lord, how profound your thoughts!*

- Not only does reflection fill us with joy, but it also makes us glad. In 2 Timothy 1:12 KJV, Paul writes about the reason for remembering when he says: *I know whom I have believed, and am persuaded that he is able to keep that which I have committed unto him against that day.*

• Perhaps no passage speaks to the joy of remembering better than Hebrews 12:1-3 NIV: *Therefore, since we are surrounded by such a great cloud of witnesses, let us throw off everything that hinders and the sin that so easily entangles. And let us run with perseverance the race marked out for us, fixing our eyes on Jesus, the pioneer and perfecter of faith. For the joy set before him he endured the cross, scorning its shame, and sat down at the right hand of the throne of God. Consider him who endured such opposition from sinners, so that you will not grow weary and lose heart.*

8. *Joy comes when people see Christ in us, and do not involve us in their ungodly actions.*

• This may sound like a strange principle, yet it has real validity. Quite often we feel badly when we are left out of activities, thinking that there is something wrong with us. But is it possible that they leave us out because there is something right about us?

• David spoke of those with evil motives when he said: *Even though powerful princes conspire against me, I fix my mind on what you require. Yes, Your testimonies are my joy; they are like the friends I seek for counsel* (my paraphrase) Psalm 119:23-24.

• Even when David's enemies were hunting him and closing in, he was able to compose joyful psalms of praise to God. He rejoiced in his understanding that God, His Father, could flatten any army, resolve any conflict and confuse the plans of those who sought to kill him. He was joyful in the Lord.

• A similar situation of opposition is explained in Acts 13:49-52 NCV: *The message of the Lord was spreading through the whole country. But the Jewish people stirred up some of the important religious women and the leaders of the city. They started trouble against Paul and Barnabas and forced them out of their area. So Paul and Barnabas shook the dust off their feet and went to Iconium. But the followers were filled with joy and the Holy Spirit.*

• There are other instances where Paul encouraged people who were insulted or rejected because of their faith. He always encouraged them to be joyful because they were suffering on behalf of Christ. Celebrate joyfully when people reject you because of your faith. You are being excluded because they see Jesus living in you according to 1 Peter 4:12-14.

Back to our story...

When I was a young man, the car I owned had a small electrical problem. I diagnosed the problem, and I went to a local department store to purchase the part that needed replacing.

I returned home only to discover after connecting the part, that it was not the problem. I determined that a small electrical fuse that only cost a few cents to replace was the problem. I had a spare fuse in my toolbox and did not need the part I had purchased.

I returned the part to the store expecting to receive the money I had paid for it. They refused to give me my money back, saying they did not give refunds on electrical parts.

I was angry and told them I would never step foot into their store again. I created a real problem for myself. I had made the statement that I would never set foot in that store again and it was the only big box department store in town. In order to keep my word, I never shopped there again, although it created a great deal of inconvenience for me. I sold my joy pretty cheaply, but in the end, it was an expensive personal lesson learned.

Do not sell your joy for any price. Do not let situations or individuals steal your joy. You hold the key that unlocks the door to your joy. Keep it locked up and do not let anyone or anything take it from you.

What kind of pastor do your people want? They want a pastor who is joyful and stirs up the joy in them also. *Rejoice in the Lord always: and again I say, Rejoice* Philippians 4:4 KJV.

Practice Personal Evangelism

Daktari Roy, do you have time to talk with me? I met John O... on my second trip to Kenya in 2013. I preached/taught at a pastors and church leaders conference he had planned and organized in Kisumu, Kenya on the shores of Lake Victoria in East Africa.

I spoke 16 times in 5 days and focused on training pastors and church leaders on the importance and 'how to' of personal evangelism. Over 300 participants from several denominations attended the conference. I sensed that Pastor John's focus was more on orphanages than evangelism and pastoral training. Boy, was I mistaken!

It was 2016, and I had not seen John in almost three years. We sat down in the lobby of my hotel, Le Savanna Hotel in Kisumu, and he began to tell me a story that was exciting and almost unbelievable.

I will recount this exciting story at the end of this chapter....

Christ is the *only means* of salvation for everyone. Acts 4:12 makes it clear that *there is salvation in no one else, for there is no other name under heaven given among men by which we must be saved.*

This statement is a reminder of Jesus' declaration in John 14:6 that He is *the way, the truth, the life and if anyone is to have access to God the father, that access can come only through Him.* There is no other way! Jesus is the only means of salvation, and He is available to every person around the world.

God *chose this method* to reach the world. When Jesus ascended back to heaven after his resurrection, he gave specific instructions to his followers regarding how others would learn about Him. In Acts 1:8, Jesus said *you will receive power when the Holy Spirit has come upon you, and you will be my witnesses in Jerusalem and in all Judea and Samaria, and to the end of the earth.*

Those instructions resulted in the spreading of the gospel around the world. This God-chosen method has remained unchanged for over 2,000 years. Personal evangelism is the *best hope* for our modern world. In Ephesians 2:14-22, Paul tells us that Jesus *is our peace, who made both groups into one and broke* down the barrier of the dividing wall, by abolishing in His flesh the enmity, which is the Law of commandments contained in ordinances, so that in Himself He might make the two into one new man, thus establishing peace, and might reconcile them both in one body to God through the cross, by it having put to death the enmity. He came and preached peace to you who were far away, and peace to those who were near; for through Him we both have our access in one Spirit to the Father.

So then you are no longer strangers and aliens, but you are fellow citizens with the saints, and are of God's household, having been built on the foundation of the apostles and prophets, Christ Jesus Himself being the corner stone, in whom the whole building, being fitted together, is growing into a holy temple in the Lord, in whom you also are being built together into a dwelling of God in the Spirit.

The world is seeking personal, community, national and international peace. The best hope for our world is the peace offered through Jesus Christ. Peace can only be found when one is at peace with himself. The only way we can find true inner peace is when we have peace with God. Since the only means of salvation is through Jesus Christ, then peace with

God may only be found through faith in His Son.

The best hope for our world today is the engagement of Christians, one-on-one with the world around us, sharing our faith in Jesus Christ. Personal evangelism is by far the best hope for our modern world.

Ethical Reasons

Christ showed us compassion; we must show that same compassion to others. Matthew 9:36-38 tells us when Jesus saw the crowds, *he had compassion for them, because they were harassed and helpless, like sheep without a shepherd. Then He said to his disciples, the harvest is plentiful, but the laborers are few; therefore pray earnestly to the Lord of the harvest to send out laborers into his harvest.*

Someone cared enough to share the good news of salvation through Jesus Christ with us. Christ's compassion was extended to us through them. Therefore, we should share that same compassion with others.

It would be selfish on our part to hide the wonderful light received and fail to give its glow to others. Sharing the gospel is the right thing to do. In Mark 16:15, Jesus instructs us to *go all over the world and share the gospel with everyone*. This is not a request by Jesus. This is a command. We are to *go and proclaim* the gospel to the whole creation.

Practical Reasons

Some people can only be reached through *personal evangelism*. They will not attend church, and their main contact with Christ will come through interaction with those who have Christ in their lives. The only hope they have for salvation is the obedience of believers who are prompted by the Holy Spirit to share the Gospel with them. This truth places a high level of responsibility and urgency on the shoulders of believers.

Other methods of evangelism such as event evangelism, neighborhood outreach, street evangelism, evangelistic crusades and relational evangelism swing on the hinge of personal evangelism. The one-to-one interaction of personal evangelism is necessary at some point, regardless of the approach to evangelization. It has been proven that churches that fail to become involved in personal evangelism will die in two generations.

I was not sure what Pastor John wanted to say to me. He had connected with another pastor from

Oklahoma, and I had connected with a totally new group in Kisumu since our time together three years before.

John began by thanking me for coming to Kisumu in 2013. He told me a story that made my heart rejoice and excited my spirit. He asked, *Do you remember teaching how to lead others to Jesus Christ? Well, God has done a great work since you were here.*

I asked him what God had done. He began to give details of God's miraculous hand and a replication of the New Testament model of personal evangelism.

He said, *Daktari Roy, when you were here in 2013, we had 14 churches in Kisumu and the adjoining regions. We now have 40 churches.*

I wanted to make sure I understood correctly what he had just said, so I asked, *26 new churches have begun in less than three years?* He responded that 26 new churches had begun in less than three years.

I asked him what the key factors were to such phenomenal growth in churches. It was personal evangelism! He told me that the pastors and leaders had put into practice the training they had received in how to lead others to Christ. Their approach was to go into villages, communities and cities and talk with people one-on-one to share the good news of the gospel. They would win them and others to Christ and begin a new church. This had been done at least 26 times in less than three years.

He also told me that these pastors were replicating their training with others who, in turn, were also becoming soul winners. He added that he personally had been and was continuing to train young pastors on a weekly basis on how to share the gospel and win others to Christ.

Personal evangelism works!

Be Responsible to Other Ministers

Did you hear about......? Unfortunately, ministers too often speak those words with their peers about other ministers. Ministry has become much more difficult with each passing year. The culture is changing and so is the respect for ministers. Pastors desperately need the special support and encouragement that other pastors and ministers can provide.

(Original story from *Our Daily Bread*, October 2, 1992)

I read a true story about a man named John. He was driving home late one night when he picked up a hitchhiker. John became suspicious of his passenger as they rode along. John checked to see if his wallet was safe in the pocket of his coat that lay on the seat between them. It was not there! He slammed on the brakes, ordered the hitchhiker out, and said, *Hand over the wallet immediately*!

The frightened hitchhiker handed over a wallet, and John drove off. When he arrived home, he started telling his wife about the experience, but she interrupted him by saying...

I will tell you the rest of the story at the end of the chapter.

Pastors' Ethical Guidelines

Below are several principles that can guide pastors in how they should treat other ministers/pastors.

1.   *Treat other ministers with respect.* We must appreciate other ministers as partners in the work of God, especially those with whom we serve in our churches. We can do this by showing proper respect for them and their ministries. We have our ministries, and they have their ministries. We should treat them like we want to be treated. God called other ministers just as he called us, and that alone requires us to appreciate them as partners in the work of God. Never treat them or their ministries as inferior to you or your ministries.

2.   *Work with other ministers when you can.* Working with other ministers on local, state and national matters is sometimes necessary. The guiding principle for me was always what was morally right and what was best for my congregation.

Working with other ministers for the moral good of the community and in the best interest of your church is something you should consider. Be careful of your reputation and be careful not to become overly involved. Remember, your primary responsibility is to your congregation.

3.   *Be careful with ministerial alliances.* I chose not to become involved with the local ministerial alliances in the cities where I pastored. I am not saying that you should not become part of these groups, but I chose not to. These organizations often are made of some religious groups that biblically I have to be diametrically opposed to because of their doctrines, biblical beliefs or practices. To me it is a matter of principle, and so I chose not to become a member.

4.   *Seek to be a blessing to other ministers and their families.* Our colleagues and their families

need our love and support. We all need each other. There are a number of ways we can do this.

One the greatest things you can do for another minister is become a friend to whom he can talk. Ministers cannot share personal things with members of their congregations. They need someone with whom they can open up and share their hearts.

A second thing you can do is to provide counsel. Many times, ministers simply need a sounding board to hear the way their own words make it from their minds, through the mouths and into their own ears. You may be a tremendous help by simply letting them bounce situations and possible solutions off you. They may want your input and suggestions. They may want your evaluation of their thinking for a solution to a particular problem. Provide counsel when requested. Be honest and open with them, but only enter doors of discussion that they clearly open to you.

A third thing you can do is stay in touch. An occasional phone call, a monthly lunch appointment, a quick text or email or a visit to their office will mean a great deal to another minister. Knowing they have a friend and fellow minister who cares and can be counted on is both encouraging and comforting.

5.   *Don't treat other pastors as competitors.*
Ego and pride are archenemies of every pastor. We must keep our guard up and make sure we do not allow our minds to travel down the road of comparison and inadequacy. Equating success or failure based on others' accomplishments is a pastoral train wreck waiting to happen.

Be careful about competing with another pastor to get a church. God will provide the ministry in which He wants you to serve. Trying to outmaneuver another pastor in order to get a church is unethical and just plain wrong.

Do not try to make yourself look good at the expense of making other pastors look bad. Enough said!

6.   *Refrain from speaking badly about the work of other pastors.* It is easy to find fault with others. Be careful not to repeat second-hand information about a fellow pastor. Sometimes we repeat unsubstantiated gossip about other pastors in an unconscious attempt to make us feel better about ourselves. This is not only wrong, but it is also sinful.

Even if the information is true, it is better not to

spread it to others. What good will it accomplish to stir the coals of destructive words that may permanently consume another's reputation? You may believe it to be true, but what if you are wrong? Keep in mind the expression: *If you cannot say something good about a person, don't say anything at all.*

7. *Do not interfere in the affairs of your former pastorates.* You should not become involved in the problems and business of any church you have previously pastored. You are not close enough to the situation at hand to know all the facts, nor should you seek to learn them.

Church members of former churches I have pastored have contacted me on occasion wanting me to become involved in a present situation at their church. I quietly, but firmly let them know that it would be inappropriate for me to become involved since I was no longer their pastor.

Resist the temptation to offer opinions or suggestions. This will not be easy because you are invested in the church. You love those people and spent years pouring your life into theirs. Let your mind override your emotions and do the right thing. Do not interfere!

8.   *Contact the present pastor before returning to a former church.* You should call the pastor before returning for weddings, funerals and visiting church member friends. Courtesy requires that he not be surprised by your visit or by hearing from others that you have been in the area.

9.   *Treat former pastors with respect, courtesy and dignity.* I made a point to always recognize them publicly in our services. I would ask them to give a word of greeting to our people. On many occasions, I would ask them to preach for me if I knew far enough in advance and it did not conflict with something else going on with the church.

I am not sure if I read the expression below or heard it mentioned in one my pastoral classes, but I have tried to practice it: *Bury your predecessor in honey rather than vinegar.* People will forget many of the shortcomings of former pastors and remember mainly the good things. You should honor and highlight them, mentioning all the good you can muster. Those who loved them will love you for it!

10.   Be kind, but honest when recommending ministers to churches and other ministries. I have recommended many people for various positions. I am very careful about attaching my good name and reputation to others. Although a few recommendations went sour on me, most have proven to be good recommendations.

Occasionally, I have given less than stellar recommendations, while trying to always be honest and fair with the ministry and the individual in question. Some people will not fit well in some ministry positions. You do them and the ministry an injustice by not voicing that concern.

A good rule of thumb to follow is: *Be fair, but honest*! Trust your instincts and give the best recommendation you can in good conscience.

11.   Misconduct by a pastor should be handled appropriately. What is the best way to handle inappropriate conduct? Here are few suggestions.

• Make sure of the facts. Be careful about proceeding on rumors and innuendos.

• Be careful to whom you talk. Talking to the wrong person can inflame the situation and spread rumors.

- Make sure that things you hear are held in strictest confidence unless the matter requires they be publicly revealed.

- Take another pastor with you and talk with the individual in question. Share with him what you have heard and offer him an opportunity to share with you his side of the story.

- If the accusations are true, follow your well-established denominational or ecclesiastical protocol to address the situation.

- Do not shoot your wounded pastor friend! Seek to help reconcile him and do your best to help restore him to whatever level in the ministry that may be possible.

Our Daily Bread, October 2, 1992

John was driving home late one night when he picked up a hitchhiker. As they rode along, he began to be suspicious of his passenger. John checked to see if his wallet was safe in the pocket of his coat that lay on the seat between them. It wasn't there! He slammed on the brakes, ordered the hitchhiker out, and said, "*Hand over the wallet immediately!*"

The frightened hitchhiker handed over a wallet, and John drove off. When John arrived home, he started to tell his wife about the experience, but she interrupted him; *John, before I forget, did you know that you left your wallet at home this morning*?

John had assumed the worst and acted accordingly. His facts were wrong, and he falsely accused and mistreated the hitchhiker. He committed the same offense of stealing the wallet of which he had falsely accused the hitchhiker.

Treating our fellow pastors with respect, dignity and courtesy is the biblically correct thing to do. In every situation, treat them the way you would want to be treated. Put yourself in their places and think about how you would want them to treat you.

If you will follow the suggestions mentioned above, you should do well in faithfully carrying out your responsibilities to you fellow pastors.

Final Chapter

You can become the pastor your people need and want you to be. Ask God to help you daily, and He will.

www.ingramcontent.com/pod-product-compliance
Lightning Source LLC
Chambersburg PA
CBHW060940040426
42445CB00011B/939